Kinky Cookies

Kinky Cookies

JOANNA FARROW

spruce

An Hachette UK Company
First published in Great Britain in 2010 by Spruce
a division of Octopus Publishing Group Ltd
Endeavour House, 189 Shaftesbury Avenue, London, WC2H 8JY
www.octopusbooks.co.uk

ISBN 13: 978-1-84601-404-8

A CIP catalogue record for this book is available
from the British Library.

Printed and bound in China

10 9 8 7 6 5 4 3 2 1

Contents

Introduction

Kinky Cookies brings a highly creative, kitsch and quirky twist to the popular trend for baking. These cookies are perfect when you want to introduce a little light-hearted fun to a variety of different occasions, such as hen parties, girls' nights, Valentine's day or simply a cosy night in. Some are easy to make and decorate, while others require more creative decorating skills such as painting, piping and intricate modelling of icing. The recipes are all designed to make about ten cookies, though you might produce more of some of the designs. You might like to bake and decorate ten of the same or maybe you'd find it more interesting and fun to mix and match a few or your favourites using the same batch of dough.

Check through your chosen recipe before you start baking to make sure you've got the necessary equipment and ingredients (see below). Some recipes require setting or hardening for several hours or overnight before you apply finishing touches, so be sure to read through the instructions well in advance.

When it comes to painting cookies (see Forbidden Fruit, page 36, and Food of Love, page 56), you might find it helpful to copy a picture or the real thing to get the finished result just right. Use the same approach with food colourings that you would with paints, mixing and blending colours to achieve the most realistic results. With time and a little patience, all the cookies in this book really can be mini works of art.

Buying ingredients

A good cake decorating shop will stock all the ingredients and equipment you can't get in the supermarket, including a good range of coloured icings and cutters. Alternatively, check out the Internet for mail-order supplies.

Using cutters and templates

Cutters for cookies and decorations, such as hearts and flowers, come in a wide range of shapes and sizes. Inexpensive and easy to use, they're worth buying when you see shapes you like. This book uses basic round, heart and star-shaped cutters. For other shapes, templates are supplied on pages 92–95. Simply trace them on to baking parchment (or lightweight paper), cut out and lay them on the rolled-out dough or icing. Cut around the shape with the tip of a sharp knife, or for more intricate shapes like Pussy Galore (see page 66), use a craft scalpel to shape the curves and corners. Work on a board or tray, as scalpels can easily damage a work surface.

Tips for making and storing cookies

Cookie dough is easy to make, either in a food processor or by hand. Once blended, the soft dough should be chilled for at least an hour to firm up enough for rolling out and shaping. When the cookies come out of the oven they'll still feel quite soft and will only firm up as they cool. For this reason, leave them on the baking sheet for a couple of minutes before transferring to a wire rack.

Once cooled, you can store the cookies overnight in an airtight container if you're not ready to decorate them straight away. If conditions are right, the undecorated cookies might keep fresh for several days but generally they have a tendency to soften. If this happens, put them on an ungreased baking sheet and pop them back in the oven for a couple of minutes to firm up.

Decorated cookies will keep for a couple of days in an airtight container in a cool place. Those with soft icing or delicate decoration should be stored in a single layer, or between layers of crumpled tissue, to protect them. Don't refrigerate cookies as they'll quickly soften.

Basic Recipes

Vanilla Cookie Dough

225 g (7½ oz) plain flour
150 g (5 oz) firm, lightly salted butter, diced
100 g (3½ oz) icing sugar
2 egg yolks
2 teaspoons vanilla bean paste or extract
MAKES about ten 7.5 cm (3¼ inch) round cookies

1 Put the flour and butter in a food processor and blend until the mixture resembles fine breadcrumbs. Briefly blend in the sugar. Add the egg yolks and vanilla and blend again until the mixture comes together to make a smooth dough. (Alternatively, to make the dough by hand, rub the butter into the flour using your fingertips until the mixture resembles fine breadcrumbs, then add the remaining ingredients and knead into a dough.)

2 Turn the dough out on to a lightly floured surface and knead gently to incorporate any stray crumbs. Press into a flat disc, wrap tightly in clingfilm and chill for at least 1 hour before rolling. Roll out and bake following your chosen recipe.

Chocolate Cookie Dough

Make the dough as above, replacing 40 g (1½ oz) of the flour with 40 g (1½ oz) of cocoa powder.

Hot Spice Cookie Dough

Make the dough as above, using light muscovado sugar instead of the icing sugar. Add 2 teaspoons of ground mixed spice and ½ teaspoon of hot chilli powder instead of the vanilla.

Vanilla Buttercream

75 g (3 oz) unsalted butter, softened
125 g (4 oz) icing sugar
1 teaspoon vanilla bean paste or extract
MAKES about 200 g (7 oz)

Put the butter, icing sugar and vanilla in a bowl and beat well with a hand-held electric whisk until pale and smooth. Add 1 teaspoon of hot water and beat until light and creamy.

Chocolate Buttercream

Make the buttercream as above, adding 40 g (1½ oz) of cocoa powder to the mixture before mixing.

Vodka Buttercream

Make as above, omitting the water and gradually beating in 3 tablespoons of vodka until smooth.

Chocolate Ganache

200 ml (7 fl oz) double cream
150 g (5 oz) plain chocolate, chopped
MAKES 350 g (11½ oz)

1 Heat the cream in a small saucepan until almost boiling. Pour into a bowl and stir in the chocolate. Leave for a few minutes, stirring frequently until the chocolate has completely melted.

2 Allow to cool completely, then chill until the mixture has thickened enough to spread over the cookies.

White Chocolate Ganache

Make as above, using white chocolate instead of plain chocolate.

9

Decorating Techniques

Piping bags

There are three types of piping bags: washable nylon bags, disposable plastic bags and disposable paper bags. Nylon bags must be used with metal piping nozzles, but both disposable plastic and paper bags can be used without a nozzle for piping lines and filling in large areas of icing, or with a writing nozzle for fine work. All types of piping bags can be bought from cake decorating suppliers, but paper bags are very easy to make at home. To make a bag, cut a 25 cm (10 inch) square of greaseproof paper in half to make two triangles. Place one triangle on a work surface with the long edge away from you. Lift the right-hand point and curl it over and down to meet the lower, centre point so the back of the right-hand point meets the front of the lower point to make a cone. Bring the left-hand point over and round the cone so the three points meet.

Fold the points over several times to stop the cone unravelling. Snip off the tiniest amount of the bag tip for fine piping or a larger piece for inserting a nozzle, if using. Half-fill the bag with icing and twist the open end round to seal, ready for piping.

Melting chocolate

To melt chocolate on a hob, chop the chocolate into small pieces and put in a heatproof bowl. Rest the bowl over a saucepan of very gently simmering water, making sure the base of the bowl doesn't touch the water. Once the chocolate starts to melt, turn off the heat and leave until completely melted, stirring once or twice.

Make sure no water or steam gets into the melted chocolate or the texture will be spoilt.

To melt chocolate in the microwave, chop the chocolate into small pieces and put in a microwave-proof bowl. Melt on full power in 30-second bursts, stirring frequently and removing from the microwave once the chocolate has almost melted. It will finish melting in the residual heat. Take care when melting

milk chocolate or white chocolate as they have a higher sugar content and are more likely to scorch.

Colouring ready-to-roll icing

Colour can be kneaded into white ready-to-roll icing so you can make the required colour and shade at home. Dust a surface with icing sugar and lightly knead the icing to soften it a little. Dot paste or liquid colouring on to the icing with a cocktail stick (or sprinkle powder on to the icing) and knead in until you have the required colour. Initially the colour will remain quite streaky but will become evenly distributed with thorough kneading.

Storing icing

Royal icing and ready-to-roll icing will quickly dry out if left to stand. Once made, wrap ready-to-roll icing tightly in clingfilm to keep it soft and pliable. When rolling or moulding, always keep any icing you're not using tightly wrapped. If you have any unused royal icing, press a layer of clingfilm directly over its surface (rather than over the bowl) to keep it soft and prevent a crust forming.

Making icing ruffles

Ready-to-roll icing ruffles make highly effective and professional-looking decorations. Dust a work surface with icing sugar and thinly roll out a piece of ready-to-roll icing. Cut into strips about 1 cm (½ inch) wide. Rest a cocktail stick on the surface so it overlaps the strip slightly. Roll the stick under your fingers along the surface so the edge of the icing starts to ruffle. Keep lifting the strip of icing and re-dusting the surface so it doesn't stick. The more you roll the cocktail stick over the icing, the more ruffled the edge will be. Trim the unruffled side to leave a straight edge and position on the cookie. If securing to an icing base, paint the back of the unruffled side with a moist brush and press the unruffled edge in place. Once the strip is positioned, lift and fold the ruffles with a cocktail stick to open them up.

Shake Your Booty

Butter, for greasing • 1 quantity Hot Spice Cookie Dough (see page 8) • Flour, for dusting • 1 quantity Vodka Buttercream (see page 9) • Icing sugar, for dusting • 200 g (7 oz) deep blue ready-to-roll icing • 150 g (5 oz) flesh-coloured ready-to-roll icing • Tubes of black, red and yellow writing icing • Edible gold dusting powder • Drop of vegetable oil • edible blue glitter

One: Preheat the oven to 190°C (375°F), Gas Mark 5 and grease a large baking sheet. Roll out the cookie dough on a lightly floured surface to a thickness of 5 mm (¼ inch). Cut out rounds using a 7.5 cm (3¼ inch) cutter, rerolling the trimmings to make extra shapes.

Two: Space the cookies slightly apart on the baking sheet and bake in the preheated oven for about 15 minutes until deep golden around the edges. Leave the cookies on the baking sheet for 2 minutes to harden a little, then transfer to a wire rack to cool completely.

Three: Spread the cookies almost to the edges with the buttercream. Dust a work surface with icing sugar and roll out the blue icing to a thickness of about 2.5 mm (⅛ inch). Cut out 10 rounds using the 7.5 cm (3¼ inch) cutter, rerolling the trimmings if necessary. Place on the cookies and press down gently.

Four: Roll out half the flesh-coloured icing in the same way and cut out 10 more rounds with the cutter. Cut out a deep V-shape from one side of each round and a gently curving shape from the other to form the figure. Gather up the trimmings and shape into pea-sized balls. Transfer the figure shapes to the cookies and press down gently, tucking two balls of icing under the top edge of each figure for breasts. Smooth the icing down gently and use a cocktail stick to indent a belly button.

Five: Use the tubes of black, red and yellow writing icing to pipe the costume on to the figure, adding a small piercing on the belly button. Leave for several hours to harden.

Six: Blend a little gold dusting powder with the oil to give a paint-like consistency. Use a small paintbrush to paint gold over the yellow icing. Flick blue glitter over the blue icing to finish.

A little bit lacy

Butter, for greasing • 1 quantity Vanilla Cookie Dough (see page 8) • Flour, for dusting
• 75 g (3 oz) white chocolate, melted (see page 10) • Icing sugar, for dusting
• 150 g (5 oz) pink ready-to-roll icing • 150 g (5 oz) black ready-to-roll icing
• Tube of black writing icing • 10 small pink or black bows

One: Preheat the oven to 190°C (375°F), Gas Mark 5 and grease a large baking sheet. Roll out the cookie dough on a lightly floured surface to a thickness of 5 mm (¼ inch). Cut out rectangles measuring 10x5 cm (4x2 inches), rerolling the trimmings to make extra shapes.

Two: Space the cookies slightly apart on the baking sheet and bake in the preheated oven for about 15 minutes until turning golden around the edges. Leave the cookies on the baking sheet for 2 minutes to harden a little, then transfer to a wire rack to cool completely.

Three: Work on a couple of cookies at a time so the chocolate doesn't harden before you have stuck the icing in place, and the icing doesn't dry out before you have time to use it. First spread the cookies almost to the edges with melted chocolate.

Four: Dust a work surface with icing sugar and thinly roll out a little pink icing. Keep the remaining icing tightly wrapped in clingfilm to prevent it drying out while you work. Cut out 4 strips for each cookie, measuring 8x1 cm (3¼x½ inch). Ruffle one edge of each strip (see page 11). Arrange one strip on each long side of the cookie with the ruffled edges facing outwards.

Five: Roll out a little black icing and make 2 ruffles for each cookie in the same way. Position on the cookies, slightly overlapping the pink ruffles. Finish with 2 more pink ruffles, leaving a narrow space along the centres of the cookies.

Six: Roll out more black icing and cut out 10 strips measuring 12x1.5 cm (5x¾ inch). Arrange the strips along the centres of the cookies, gathering them up slightly as you work to give a ruffled appearance. Pipe small dots of black writing icing along the edges of the gathered strips and use the icing to secure bows to the centres.

In Chains

Icing sugar, for dusting • 100 g (3½ oz) grey ready-to-roll icing • Butter, for greasing • 1 quantity Chocolate Cookie Dough (see page 8) • Flour, for dusting • Edible silver and pink dusting powders • Drop of vegetable oil • 1 quantity Chocolate Ganache (see page 9)

One: Line a small tray or baking sheet with baking parchment. Dust a work surface with icing sugar and roll out the grey icing to a thickness of about 2.5 mm (⅛ inch). Cut out rounds using a 3.5 cm (1½ inch) cutter. Transfer to the baking parchment and cut out the centres using a 2.5 cm (1 inch) cutter to make rings.

Two: Reroll the trimmings and cut out an equal number of rectangles measuring 4x1 cm (1½x½ inch). Taper the rectangles to points at the ends and secure a strip to the side of each ring using a dampened paintbrush. Push a 'keyhole' into the centre of each with a skewer.

Three: To make the chains, roll tiny balls of icing, about the size of a small pea. Flatten each of the balls on the baking parchment and push a hole in the centre with the skewer. You'll need about 7 balls for each cookie. Reroll the trimmings and cut out small key shapes, each about 2x1 cm (¾x½ inch). Leave all the decorations to harden for several hours or overnight.

Four: Preheat the oven to 190°C (375°F), Gas Mark 5 and grease a large baking sheet. Roll out the cookie dough on a lightly floured surface to a thickness of 5 mm (¼ inch). Cut out rounds using a 7.5 cm (3¼ inch) cutter, rerolling the trimmings to make extra shapes.

Five: Space the cookies slightly apart on the baking sheet and bake in the preheated oven for about 15 minutes until turning darker around the edges. Leave the cookies on the baking sheet for 2 minutes to harden a little, then transfer to a wire rack to cool completely.

Six: Blend a little silver dusting powder with the oil to give a paint-like consistency. Use a small paintbrush to paint all the grey icing decorations and allow to dry. Spread the cookies to the edges with chocolate ganache and arrange the icing shapes on top. Sprinkle with the pink dusting powder to finish.

Kinky Boots

Butter, for greasing • 1 quantity Hot Spice Cookie Dough (see page 8) • Flour, for dusting • 300 g (10 oz) royal icing sugar • Black and deep red food colourings

One: Trace the Kinky Boots shape on page 94 and use to make a template. Preheat the oven to 190°C (375°F), Gas Mark 5 and grease a large baking sheet. Roll out the cookie dough on a lightly floured surface to a thickness of 5 mm (¼ inch). Cut out shapes by cutting round the template with a sharp knife or scalpel, rerolling the trimmings to make extra shapes.

Two: Space the cookies slightly apart on the baking sheet and bake in the preheated oven for about 15 minutes until deep golden around the edges. Leave the cookies on the baking sheet for 2 minutes to harden a little, then transfer to a wire rack to cool completely.

Three: Put the royal icing sugar in a bowl and add enough water, about 3 tablespoons, to mix to a smooth paste. Spoon one-third into a separate bowl and beat in the black food colouring.

Put half of the black icing into a piping bag fitted with a writing nozzle and cover the rest tightly with clingfilm to prevent a crust forming. Beat the red food colouring into the remaining icing and add a dash of water to give a slightly looser consistency. Put in a piping bag and snip off the tip so the icing flows quite freely.

Four: Use the black icing to pipe a line around the edges of the boots. Pipe further lines to make platform soles. Use the red icing to fill in the centres of the boots, easing the icing into the corners with a cocktail stick. Leave to set for several hours or overnight.

Five: Put the reserved black icing in a piping bag fitted with a writing nozzle and use to pipe around the edges of the boots again over the initial line, then add the detail at the tops of the boots and the laces.

In Need of Nursing

Butter, for greasing • 1 quantity Hot Spice Cookie Dough (see page 8)
• Flour, for dusting • Icing sugar, for dusting • 100 g (3½ oz) white ready-to-roll icing
• 1 quantity Vodka Buttercream (see page 9) • Tubes of black and white writing icing
• Red and black food colourings • Large edible silver balls

One: Preheat the oven to 190°C (375°F), Gas Mark 5 and grease a large baking sheet. Roll out the cookie dough on a lightly floured surface to a thickness of 5 mm (¼ inch). Cut out figures using a 12 or 13 cm (5 or 5½ inch) gingerbread man cutter, rerolling the trimmings to make extra shapes.

Two: Space the cookies slightly apart on the baking sheet and bake in the preheated oven for about 15 minutes until deep golden around the edges. Leave the cookies on the baking sheet for 2 minutes to harden a little, then transfer to a wire rack to cool completely.

Three: Dust a work surface with icing sugar and roll out the white icing to a thickness of about 2.5 mm (⅛ inch). Cut out nurse's dresses and secure in place on the cookies with buttercream. This is easy to do using the gingerbread man cutter, then cutting off the excess areas. Reroll the trimmings as necessary.

Four: Use the black writing icing to make the hair. Next cut out small hats from the white icing and press gently on to the hair. Use the red food colouring and a fine paintbrush to paint a cross on each hat, the lips, cleavages and belts on the cookies.

Five: Pipe along the edges of the belt with black writing icing, then press the silver balls in place along the belts. Use the white writing icing to pipe fishnet stockings on the legs, then add suspenders and shoes in black writing icing. Finally paint the eyes using black food colouring.

Between the Sheets

Butter, for greasing • 1 quantity Chocolate Cookie Dough (see page 8) • Flour, for dusting • Icing sugar, for dusting • 150 g (5 oz) pink ready-to-roll icing • 100 g (3½ oz) purple ready-to-roll icing • 50 g (2 oz) black ready-to-roll icing • 50 g (2 oz) flesh-coloured ready-to-roll icing • Flesh-coloured food colouring • 100 g (3½ oz) milk or plain chocolate, melted (see page 10) • Edible silver dusting powder • Drop of vegetable oil

One: Preheat the oven to 190°C (375°F), Gas Mark 5 and grease a large baking sheet. Roll out the cookie dough on a lightly floured surface to a thickness of 5 mm (¼ inch). Cut out rectangles measuring 10x5 cm (4x2 inches), rerolling the trimmings to make extra shapes.

Two: Space the cookies slightly apart on the baking sheet and bake in the preheated oven for about 15 minutes until turning darker around the edges. Leave the cookies on the baking sheet for 2 minutes to harden a little, then transfer to a wire rack to cool completely.

Three: Dust a work surface with icing sugar and thinly roll out the pink icing. Cut out rectangles measuring 10x2.5 cm (4x1 inch), cover with clingfilm and set aside. Thinly roll out the purple and black icings. Cut the black icing into very thin strips and lay them on top of the purple icing to create parallel stripes. Gently roll with the rolling pin to incorporate the two icings. Cut into pieces, each about 12x4 cm (5x1½ inches). Cover with clingfilm and set aside.

Four: Take half the flesh-coloured icing and knead in a little flesh-coloured food colouring to darken the shade. Take a large pea-sized piece of the icing and use your fingers to mould it into a foot shape. Repeat to make 2 pale feet and 2 darker feet for each cookie.

Five: Spread a little melted chocolate along the lower half of each cookie and in the centre of the top half (where the feet will be). Arrange the rectangles of pink icing over the lower halves of the cookies and indent lines with the back of a knife. Now lightly scrunch up the stripy icing strips and press on to the chocolate on the top halves of the cookies to make sheets, leaving a gap in the middle for the feet. Press the feet into position in the melted chocolate.

Six: Blend a little silver dusting powder with the oil to give a paint-like consistency. Use a small paintbrush to paint a toe ring on one of the feet on each cookie.

Long Lashes

Butter, for greasing • 1 quantity Vanilla Cookie Dough (see page 8) • Flour, for dusting
• 1 quantity Vodka Buttercream (see page 9) • Icing sugar, for dusting
• 250 g (8 oz) flesh-coloured ready-to-roll icing • 50 g (2 oz) white ready-to-roll icing
• Blue dusting powder • Blue, brown and black food colourings

One: Preheat the oven to 190°C (375°F), Gas Mark 5 and grease a large baking sheet. Roll out the cookie dough on a lightly floured surface to a thickness of 5 mm (¼ inch). Cut out rounds using a 7.5 cm (3¼ inch) cutter, rerolling the trimmings to make extra shapes. Use a rolling pin to roll each circle of dough very gently in one direction only until it is shaped like an egg.

Two: Space the cookies slightly apart on the baking sheet and bake in the preheated oven for about 15 minutes until turning golden around the edges. Leave the cookies on the baking sheet for 2 minutes to harden a little, then transfer to a wire rack to cool completely.

Three: Spread the cookies with the buttercream. Dust a work surface with icing sugar and roll out the flesh-coloured icing to a thickness of about 2.5 mm (⅛ inch). Cut out rounds using the same cutter, then use the same technique to roll the rounds into egg

Four: Trace the Long Lashes shape on page 94 and use to make a template. Thinly roll out the white icing and cut out shapes by cutting round the template with a sharp knife or scalpel, rerolling the trimmings to make extra shapes if necessary. Wet the backs of the shapes with a dampened paintbrush, position on the cookies and leave to harden for several hours or overnight.

Five: Use your finger to press the blue dusting powder around the tops of the eyes and a little underneath for eye shadow. Use a fine paintbrush and diluted blue food colouring to paint the irises of the eyes. Add a dark brown circle in the middle for the pupil. Use brown food colouring to paint the eye brows and black to paint the eyeliner and false lashes.

Forbidden Pearl

Butter, for greasing • 1 quantity Hot Spice Cookie Dough (see page 8) • Flour, for dusting • 2 quantities Vodka Buttercream (see page 9) • Black and brown food colourings • 300 g (10 oz) white ready-to-roll icing • Icing sugar, for dusting • Edible pearl-coloured dusting powder

One: Trace the Forbidden Pearl shape on page 92 and use to make a template. Preheat the oven to 190°C (375°F), Gas Mark 5 and grease a large baking sheet. Roll out the cookie dough on a lightly floured surface to a thickness of 5 mm (¼ inch). Cut out shapes by cutting round the template with a sharp knife or scalpel, rerolling the trimmings to make extra shapes.

Two: Space the cookies slightly apart on the baking sheet and bake in the preheated oven for about 15 minutes until deep golden around the edges. Leave the cookies on the baking sheet for 2 minutes to harden a little, then transfer to a wire rack to cool completely.

Three: Transfer 5 tablespoons of the buttercream to a separate bowl, colour it with black food colouring and put it in a piping bag fitted with a writing nozzle. Spread the remainder of the buttercream over the cookies, doming it up in the centre where the oyster meat would be.

Four: Knead a drop of black food colouring into the white ready-to-roll icing to colour it the palest shade of grey. Dust a work surface with icing sugar and roll out the icing to a thickness of about 2.5 mm (⅛ inch). Cut out oyster shapes slightly larger than the cookies, using the template as a guide. Position on the cookies, moulding the icing gently over the mound of buttercream and moulding the excess icing up around the sides of the cookies to give a slightly raised edge.

Five: Use the icing trimmings to make small balls for the pearls, then roll them in dusting powder to coat and set aside. Rub more dusting powder around the outer edges of the shells using your fingers. Use the remainder of the icing trimmings to mould flat oyster shapes and lay them over the buttercream mounds to resemble oyster meat.

Six: Use the black buttercream to pipe wriggly lines around the centres of the cookies. Draw a dampened paintbrush through the piped lines towards the centre. Paint the edges of the shells with black and brown food colouring using a small paintbrush, then add an icing pearl to each shell to finish.

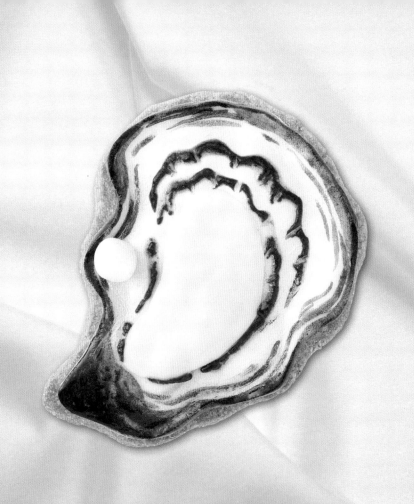

Five-Inch Heels

Butter, for greasing • 1 quantity Vanilla Cookie Dough (see page 8)
• Flour, for dusting • 300 g (10 oz) royal icing sugar • 3 tablespoons lemon juice
• Dark blue and pink food colourings • 10 small deep pink bows

One: Trace the Five-Inch Heels shape on page 95 and use to make a template. Preheat the oven to 190°C (375°F), Gas Mark 5 and grease a large baking sheet. Roll out the cookie dough on a lightly floured surface to a thickness of 5 mm (¼ inch). Cut out shapes by cutting round the template with a sharp knife or scalpel, rerolling the trimmings to make extra shapes.

Two: Space the cookies slightly apart on the baking sheet and bake in the preheated oven for about 15 minutes until turning golden around the edges. Leave the cookies on the baking sheet for 2 minutes to harden a little, then transfer to a wire rack to cool completely.

Three: Put the royal icing sugar in a bowl and add enough lemon juice to mix to a smooth paste. Spoon one-quarter of the icing into a separate bowl and cover tightly with clingfilm to prevent a crust forming. Set aside. Colour the remaining icing deep blue and put 3 tablespoons of it in a piping bag fitted with a writing nozzle. Cut around the dotted line of the stiletto template and place the cut-out section on a cookie. Pipe the blue icing around the template for an outline of the shoes.

Four: Add a dash of water to the remaining blue icing to give a slightly looser consistency. Put in a piping bag and snip off the tip so the icing flows quite freely. Use the icing to fill in the centres of the shoes, easing the icing into the corners with a cocktail stick. Leave to set for several hours or overnight.

Five: Colour the reserved icing with pink food colouring and put in a piping bag fitted with a writing nozzle. Use to pipe rows of dots along the top edge of the shoes, a line across the heel and the decorative lines over the front. Secure the bows in place with dots of icing.

Skin Deep

Butter, for greasing • 1 quantity Vanilla Cookie Dough (see page 8) • Flour, for dusting • 1 quantity Vodka Buttercream (see page 9) • Icing sugar, for dusting • 200 g (7 oz) flesh-coloured ready-to-roll icing • Red, green and black food colourings

One: Preheat the oven to 190°C (375°F), Gas Mark 5 and grease a large baking sheet. Roll out the cookie dough on a lightly floured surface to a thickness of 5 mm (¼ inch). Cut out rounds using a 7.5 cm (3¼ inch) cutter, rerolling the trimmings to make extra shapes.

Two: Space the cookies slightly apart on the baking sheet and bake in the preheated oven for about 15 minutes until turning golden around the edges. Leave the cookies on the baking sheet for 2 minutes to harden a little, then transfer to a wire rack to cool completely.

Three: Spread the cookies almost to the edges with buttercream. Dust a work surface with icing sugar and roll out the flesh-coloured icing to a thickness of about 2.5 mm (⅛ inch). Cut out rounds using the same cutter. Press gently on to the cookies and leave to harden for several hours or overnight.

Four: Use a fine paintbrush and the red food colouring to paint rose shapes towards one side of the cookies. Once the outline is complete, dilute more colouring with water and dot it around the painted red lines to resemble a tattoo. Use green food colouring to paint the leaves in the same way and diluted black colouring to paint the tendrils and thorns.

Heaven Scent

Butter, for greasing • 1 quantity Hot Spice Cookie Dough (see page 8) • Flour, for dusting • 300 g (10 oz) royal icing sugar • 2 teaspoons rosewater • Pink and black food colourings • Edible silver dusting powder • 1 m (3 ft) black ribbon, about 5 mm (¼ inch) wide

One: Trace the Heaven Scent shape on page 94 and use to make a template. Preheat the oven to 190°C (375°F), Gas Mark 5 and grease a large baking sheet. Roll out the cookie dough on a lightly floured surface to a thickness of 5 mm (¼ inch). Cut out shapes by cutting round the template with a sharp knife or scalpel, rerolling the trimmings to make extra shapes.

Two: Space the cookies slightly apart on the baking sheet and bake in the preheated oven for about 15 minutes until deep golden around the edges. Leave the cookies on the baking sheet for 2 minutes to harden a little, then transfer to a wire rack to cool completely.

Three: Put the royal icing sugar in a bowl and add the rosewater and enough water, about 2½ tablespoons, to mix to a smooth paste. Spoon 4 tablespoons of the icing into a separate bowl and beat in the black food colouring. Put the black icing into a piping bag fitted with a writing nozzle. Beat the pink food colouring into the remaining icing and add a dash of water for a looser consistency. Put in a piping bag and snip off the tip so the icing flows.

Four: Use the black icing to pipe a line around the edges of the bottles and around the spray nozzles at the top. Fill in the tops of the bottles with black piped icing. Set aside the remaining black icing in the piping bag. Use the pink icing to fill in the centres of the bottles, easing the icing into the corners with a cocktail stick. Leave to set for several hours or overnight.

Five: Use a soft paintbrush to dust silver powder around the lower halves of the cookies. Use the remaining black icing to pipe a small motif on to the bottles, such as a tiara, butterfly or someone's initials. (If the icing has set in the nozzle, spoon the icing from the bag into a bowl while you fit another bag with the cleaned nozzle). Cut the ribbon into 10 cm (4 inch) lengths and tie around the bottles, securing with double-sided tape.

Fallen Angel

Butter, for greasing • 1 quantity Vanilla Cookie Dough (see page 8) • Flour, for dusting • 2 quantities Vodka Buttercream (see page 9) • Black food colouring • Icing sugar, for dusting • Small piece of yellow ready-to-roll icing • Edible gold dusting powder • Dash of vegetable oil

One: Trace the Fallen Angel shape on page 93 and use to make a template. Preheat the oven to 190°C (375°F), Gas Mark 5 and grease a large baking sheet. Roll out the cookie dough on a lightly floured surface to a thickness of 5 mm (¼ inch). Cut out shapes by cutting round the template with a sharp knife or scalpel, rerolling the trimmings to make extra shapes.

Two: Space the cookies slightly apart on the baking sheet and bake in the preheated oven for about 15 minutes until turning golden around the edges. Leave the cookies on the baking sheet for 2 minutes to harden a little, then transfer to a wire rack to cool completely.

Three: Spoon half the buttercream into a bowl and use black food colouring to colour it a pale grey. Divide the remainder between two more bowls. Colour one bowl a slightly darker shade of grey and the third bowl darker still. Spoon the two darkest buttercreams into separate piping bags and half the pale buttercream into another bag. Snip off the merest tips of the bags.

Four: Spread the remaining pale grey buttercream over the cookies in a smooth layer, scraping off any that overhangs the edges. Use the dark grey buttercream to pipe the long, lower feathers on the wings. Use the medium shade to pipe the middle section of feathers and the palest shade to pipe the top row of feathers.

Five: Dust a work surface with icing sugar and roll the yellow icing under your fingers to make a long sausage about 5 mm (¼ inch) thick. Cut into 5 cm (2 inch) lengths and wrap one around one wing of each cookie to make a halo. Blend a little gold dusting powder with the oil to give a paint-like consistency. Use a small paintbrush to paint gold over the yellow icing.

Forbidden Fruit

Butter, for greasing • 1 quantity Hot Spice Cookie Dough (see page 8)
• Flour, for dusting • 2 tablespoons smooth apricot jam • Icing sugar, for dusting
• 375 g (12 oz) white almond paste • Purple, green and red food colourings

One: Draw a 7 cm (3 inch) circle on a piece of thick paper using a cookie cutter as a guide. Add a small, curved point on one side of the circle to make a fig shape and cut out the shape to use as a template. Preheat the oven to 190°C (375°F), Gas Mark 5 and grease a large baking sheet. Roll out the cookie dough on a lightly floured surface to a thickness of 5 mm (¼ inch). Cut out shapes by cutting round the template with a sharp knife or scalpel, rerolling the trimmings to make extra shapes.

Two: Space the cookies slightly apart on the baking sheet and bake in the preheated oven for about 15 minutes until deep golden around the edges. Leave the cookies on the baking sheet for 2 minutes to harden a little, then transfer to a wire rack to cool completely.

Three: Spread the cookies with the apricot jam. Dust a work surface with icing sugar and roll out the almond paste. Cut out fig shapes, using the template as a guide, rerolling the trimmings to make extra shapes if necessary. Transfer the shapes to the cookies and press down gently.

Four: Paint the figs using a small paintbrush and the purple, green and red food colourings, diluting the colours with water to paint the paler areas. For the best results, refer to a photograph or a fresh fig to get the colours just right.

Boobalicious

Butter, for greasing • 1 quantity Chocolate Cookie Dough (see page 8) • Flour, for dusting • 1 quantity Chocolate Buttercream (see page 9) • about 10 large soft chocolate truffles • Icing sugar, for dusting • 300 g (10 oz) flesh-coloured ready-to-roll icing • Brown food colouring

One: Preheat the oven to 190°C (375°F), Gas Mark 5 and grease a large baking sheet. Roll out the cookie dough on a lightly floured surface to a thickness of 5 mm (¼ inch). Cut out rounds using a 7.5 cm (3¼ inch) cutter, rerolling the trimmings to make extra shapes if necessary.

Two: Space the cookies slightly apart on the baking sheet and bake in the preheated oven for about 15 minutes until turning darker around the edges. Leave the cookies on the baking sheet for 2 minutes to harden a little, then transfer to a wire rack to cool completely.

Three: Spread each cookie with a thin layer of buttercream, leaving a 1 cm (½ inch) border around the edges. Cut the truffles in half and flatten each half slightly on one side. Position two truffle halves, cut sides down and flattened sides facing each other, in the centre of each cookie, leaving a 1 cm (½ inch) gap between them.

Four: Dust a work surface with icing sugar and roll out the flesh-coloured icing to a thickness of about 2.5 mm (⅛ inch). Cut out rounds using an 8 cm (3½ inch) cutter. Position them on the cookies, easing to fit around the truffles and smoothing out any uneven areas using fingers dusted with icing sugar. Trim off any excess icing around the edges of the cookies.

Five: Shape tiny nipples using the icing trimmings and secure in place with a dampened paintbrush. Paint with brown food colouring, diluted with a dash of water.

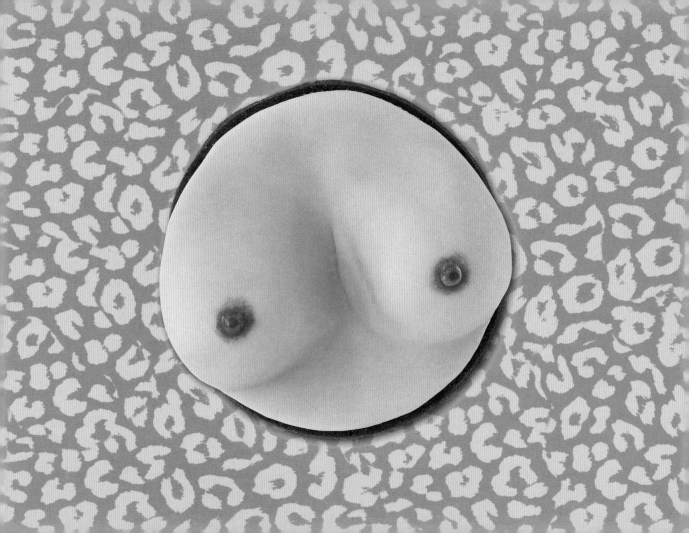

Love Bite

Butter, for greasing • 1 quantity Hot Spice Cookie Dough (see page 8) • Flour, for dusting
• Icing sugar, for dusting • 150 g (5 oz) pink ready-to-roll icing • 50 g (2 oz) black ready-to-roll icing
• 1 quantity Vanilla Buttercream (see page 9) • 50 g (2 oz) flesh-coloured ready-to-roll icing
• Tube of green writing icing • Small piece of deep red ready-to-roll icing • Clear piping gel (optional)

One: Preheat the oven to 190°C (375°F), Gas Mark 5 and grease a large baking sheet. Roll out the cookie dough on a lightly floured surface to a thickness of 5 mm (¼ inch). Cut out rounds using a 7 cm (3 inch) cutter, rerolling the trimmings to make extra shapes. Lightly roll over each round with the rolling pin to stretch it into an oval shape.

Two: Space the cookies slightly apart on the baking sheet and bake in the preheated oven for about 15 minutes until deep golden around the edges. Leave the cookies on the baking sheet for 2 minutes to harden a little, then transfer to a wire rack to cool completely.

Three: Dust a work surface with icing sugar and thinly roll out the pink and black icings. Cut the black icing into very thin strips and lay them on top of the pink icing to create parallel stripes. Gently roll with the rolling pin to incorporate the two icings. Cut out rounds using the 7 cm (3 inch) cutter and flatten into ovals as before. Wrap the black trimmings in clingfilm and set aside.

Four: Put 4 tablespoons of the buttercream in a piping bag fitted with a writing nozzle. Spread the cookies with the remaining buttercream, leaving a 1 cm (½ inch) border around the edges. Press the striped icing ovals gently on to the cookies.

Five: Trace the Love Bite shape on page 92 and use to make a template. Roll out the flesh-coloured icing and cut out shapes by cutting round the template with a sharp knife or scalpel, rerolling the trimmings to make extra shapes. Paint the backs of the shapes with a dampened paintbrush and position them on the cookies.

Six: Use the buttercream in the piping bag to pipe hair. Reroll the black icing trimmings and cut out tiny flowers using a small plunger cutter. Press into the hair and pipe dots into the centres. Pipe the cherry stalks in place using green writing icing. Roll tiny balls of red icing and position at the ends of the stalks for cherries. Paint the cherries with clear gel, if using.

Hot Lips

Butter, for greasing • 1 quantity Hot Spice Cookie Dough (see page 8) • Flour, for dusting • 300 g (10 oz) royal icing sugar • Red food colouring • Icing sugar, for dusting • 25 g (1 oz) white ready-to-roll icing • Tube of green writing icing • Confectioner's glaze or clear honey

One: Trace the Hot Lips shape on page 95 and use to make a template. Preheat the oven to 190°C (375°F), Gas Mark 5 and grease a large baking sheet. Roll out the cookie dough on a lightly floured surface to a thickness of 5 mm (¼ inch). Cut out shapes by cutting round the template with a sharp knife or scalpel, rerolling the trimmings to make extra shapes.

Two: Space the cookies slightly apart on the baking sheet and bake in the preheated oven for about 15 minutes until deep golden around the edges. Leave the cookies on the baking sheet for 2 minutes to harden a little, then transfer to a wire rack to cool completely.

Three: Put the royal icing sugar in a bowl and add enough water, about 3 tablespoons, to mix to a smooth paste. Beat in some red food colouring to make it a bright chilli red. Put 4 tablespoons of the icing into a piping bag fitted with a writing nozzle and cover the rest with clingfilm to prevent a crust forming. Using the dotted lines on the template as a guide, pipe the outline of the chilli on to the cookies. Pipe outlines for top and lower edges of the lips.

Four: Add a dash of water to the remaining icing to give a slightly looser consistency. Put half in a piping bag and snip off the tip so the icing flows quite freely. Use the icing to fill in the centres of the chillies, easing the icing into the corners with a cocktail stick. Add more red food colouring to the remaining icing to colour a deep, scarlet red. Put in a piping bag and snip off the tip.

Five: Dust a work surface with icing sugar and roll out the white icing to a thickness of about 2.5 mm (⅛ inch). Cut into thin strips and make 'tooth' indentations along one edge of each. Stick a set of teeth to each cookie, holding it in place with a little piped icing.

Six: Use the dark red icing in the piping bag to fill in the lip areas. Pipe green icing over the chilli stalks, then leave to set for several hours or overnight. Finally, brush confectioner's glaze or clear honey over the lips for a glossy sheen.

All Man

Butter, for greasing • 1 quantity Chocolate Cookie Dough (see page 8) • Flour, for dusting • Icing sugar, for dusting • 500 g (1 lb) flesh-coloured ready-to-roll icing • 75 g (3 oz) white chocolate, melted (see page 10) • Brown food colouring • 25 g (1 oz) each of white and black ready-to-roll icing • 20 edible pearls

One: Preheat the oven to 190°C (375°F), Gas Mark 5 and grease a large baking sheet. Roll out the cookie dough on a lightly floured surface to a thickness of 5 mm (¼ inch). Cut out rounds using a 7.5 cm (3¼ inch) cutter, rerolling the trimmings to make extra shapes.

Two: Space the cookies slightly apart on the baking sheet and bake in the preheated oven for about 15 minutes until turning darker around the edges. Leave the cookies on the baking sheet for 2 minutes to harden a little, then transfer to a wire rack to cool completely.

Three: Dust a work surface with icing sugar. Take a 30 g (1¼ oz) piece of flesh-coloured icing and flatten it out into a torso shape that tapers into a neck at the top and narrows to a waist at the bottom. Use the side of a fine paintbrush to impress '6 pack' markings in the icing. Repeat to make all the torsos. Spread the cookies to the edges with white chocolate, then press the torsos in place.

Four: Divide the remaining icing into equal pieces, one for each cookie. Take one piece, cut in half and shape each half into an arm, one left and one right. Repeat with the other pieces of icing. Brush the shoulders with a dampened paintbrush and press into place against the torsos. Dilute a little brown food colouring with water and use a fine paintbrush to paint the nipples and areas of shadow.

Five: Roll out the white and black icings and cut out bow ties, belts, collars and cuffs. Secure in place with a dampened paintbrush, then press the pearls into the cuffs for cuff links.

Tantalizing Tassels

Icing sugar, for dusting • 150 g (5 oz) deep pink ready-to-roll icing • Pink colouring powder • 3 tablespoons granulated sugar • Butter, for greasing • 1 quantity Vanilla Cookie Dough (see page 8) • Flour, for dusting • 1 quantity Vodka Buttercream (see page 9) • 200 g (7 oz) white almond paste • 75 g (3 oz) pale pink ready-to-roll icing • 50 g (2 oz) black ready-to-roll icing

One: Line a tray or baking sheet with baking parchment. Dust a work surface with icing sugar, and roll 20 balls of deep pink icing about the size of a large pea. Add a little pink colouring powder to the granulated sugar and work the colour into the sugar with the back of a teaspoon. Once the colour is mostly distributed, use rub the rest of the colour in. Scatter the sugar on a plate.

Two: Roll out the remaining deep pink icing to a thickness of about 4 mm (³⁄₁₆ inch) and cut out 10 heart shapes using a 5 cm (2 inch) heart-shaped cutter, rerolling the trimmings for make extra shapes. Press the heart shapes into the sugar, then rest each over a ball of icing on the parchment paper. Press gently so the heart sticks to the ball. Leave to harden for several hours.

Three: Preheat the oven to 190°C (375°F), Gas Mark 5 and grease a large baking sheet. Roll out the cookie dough on a lightly floured surface to a thickness of 5 mm (¼ inch). Cut out 10 rounds using a 7 cm (3 inch) cutter, rerolling the trimmings to make extra shapes if necessary. Space the cookies slightly apart on the baking sheet and bake in the preheated oven for about 15 minutes until turning golden around the edges. Leave the cookies on the baking sheet for 2 minutes to harden a little, then transfer to a wire rack to cool completely.

Four: Spread the cookies with buttercream. Knead pink food colouring into the almond paste until it is an even pink colour. Dust a work surface with icing sugar and roll it out very thinly. Cut out 10 rounds using the 7 cm (3 inch) cutter. Position on the cookies, pressing gently. Roll out the pale pink icing and cut into 1 cm (½ inch) wide strips long enough to wrap around the cookies. Dampen the edges of the marzipan and secure the strips of icing, trimming the ends where they meet.

Five: Position the hearts on top of the cookies, holding in place by brushing the balls with a damp brush. Roll out the black icing thinly and cut out 20 5x3 cm (2x1¼ inches) rectangles. Make a series of deep cuts in the rectangles, keeping them intact at one short end. Roll up to form tassels and position on the hearts. Use the trimmings to make 20 tiny balls and place one at the top of each tassel.

Babydoll

1 quantity Vanilla Cookie Dough (see page 8) • Flour, for dusting
• 75 g (3 oz) clear red boiled sweets, roughly crushed • 200 g (7 oz) royal icing sugar
• Black food colouring • Edible silver dusting powder • Dash of vegetable oil

One: Trace the Babydoll shape on page 94 and use to make a template. Preheat the oven to 190°C (375°F), Gas Mark 5 and line a large baking sheet with baking parchment. Roll out the cookie dough on a lightly floured surface to a thickness of 5 mm (¼ inch). Cut out rounds using an 8.5 cm (3½ inch) fluted-edged cutter, rerolling the trimmings to make extra shapes.

Two: Place the template over a cookie and cut around it with a sharp knife or scalpel. Lift out the centre and repeat with the other cookies. Reroll the centres to make extra cookies. Space the cookies slightly apart on the baking sheet and bake in the preheated oven for 5 minutes. Divide the crushed sweets between the holes in the cookies and return to the oven for about 8 minutes or until the cookies are turning golden around the edges. If necessary, use a cocktail stick to spread the melted syrup into any areas that haven't been filled, then leave to cool completely on the baking sheet.

Three: Carefully peel the parchment away from the cookies and place them on a clean sheet of parchment. Put the royal icing sugar in a bowl and add enough water, about 2 tablespoons, to mix to a smooth paste. Beat in black food colouring and transfer to a piping bag fitted with a writing nozzle. Use to pipe an outline around the edges of the baby doll shapes and little straps and bows at the shoulders. Fill in with further piping, using the picture as a guide. Add rows of tiny dots along the top and bottom of each babydoll. Leave to harden for several hours.

Four: Blend a little silver dusting powder with the oil to give a paint-like consistency. Use a small paintbrush to paint silver over the shoulder straps and dotted edges.

Bubble Love

Butter, for greasing • 1 quantity Hot Spice Cookie Dough (see page 8) • Flour, for dusting
• Pink colouring powder • 150 g (5 oz) white chocolate, melted (see page 10) • 1 quantity Vodka
Buttercream (see page 9) • Blue food colouring • Tubes of red and black writing icing
• Icing sugar, for dusting • 50 g (2 oz) each of yellow and brown ready-to-roll icing

One: Trace the Bubble Love shape on page 95 and use to make a template. Preheat the oven to 190°C (375°F), Gas Mark 5 and grease a large baking sheet. Roll out the cookie dough on a lightly floured surface to a thickness of 5 mm (¼ inch). Cut out shapes by cutting round the template with a sharp knife or scalpel, rerolling the trimmings to make extra shapes.

Two: Space the cookies slightly apart on the baking sheet and bake in the preheated oven for about 15 minutes until deep golden around the edges. Leave the cookies on the baking sheet for 2 minutes to harden a little, then transfer to a wire rack to cool completely.

Three: Line a tray or baking sheet with baking parchment. Beat a little pink colouring powder into the white chocolate. Use a teaspoon to coat the bath areas of the cookies in chocolate, letting the excess fall back into the bowl. Scrape off the drips around the edges and transfer to the tray to harden.

Four: Colour the buttercream pale blue and put in a piping bag fitted with a writing nozzle. Use to pipe dots all along the tops of the baths to resemble bubbles, building the dots up in layers as you go. Use the red writing icing to pipe kissing lips and the black to pipe closed eyes.

Five: Dust a work surface with icing sugar and roll out the yellow and brown icing thinly. Cut out hair shapes with the tip of a sharp knife or scalpel and secure in place with buttercream.

Kissable Cheeks

Butter, for greasing • 1 quantity Vanilla Cookie Dough (see page 8) • Flour, for dusting
• Red colouring powder • 1 quantity White Chocolate Ganache (see page 9)
• Icing sugar, for dusting • 750 g (1½ lb) flesh-coloured ready-to-roll icing • Red food colouring

One: Preheat the oven to 190°C (375°F), Gas Mark 5 and grease a large baking sheet. Roll out the cookie dough on a lightly floured surface to a thickness of 5 mm (¼ inch). Cut out rounds using a 7.5 cm (3¼ inch) cutter, rerolling the trimmings to make extra shapes.

Two: Space the cookies slightly apart on the baking sheet and bake in the preheated oven for about 15 minutes until turning golden around the edges. Leave the cookies on the baking sheet for 2 minutes to harden a little, then transfer to a wire rack to cool completely.

Three: Beat a little red colouring powder into the white chocolate ganache and spread it on the cookies. Dust a work surface with icing sugar. Take a 50 g (2 oz) piece of flesh-coloured icing, roll it into a ball and cut in half. Flatten the two halves slightly then arrange on a cookie, pushing them together to resemble a bottom. Repeat with the other cookies.

Four: Roll out the remainder of the flesh-coloured icing thinly. Cut out rounds using a 7.5 cm (3¼ inch) cutter. Lay over the cookies, smoothing out any creases with your fingers and using a sharp knife to make a cut between the cheeks. Trim off any excess around the edges. Use a fine paintbrush and red food colouring to paint a lipstick kiss on to the cheeks.

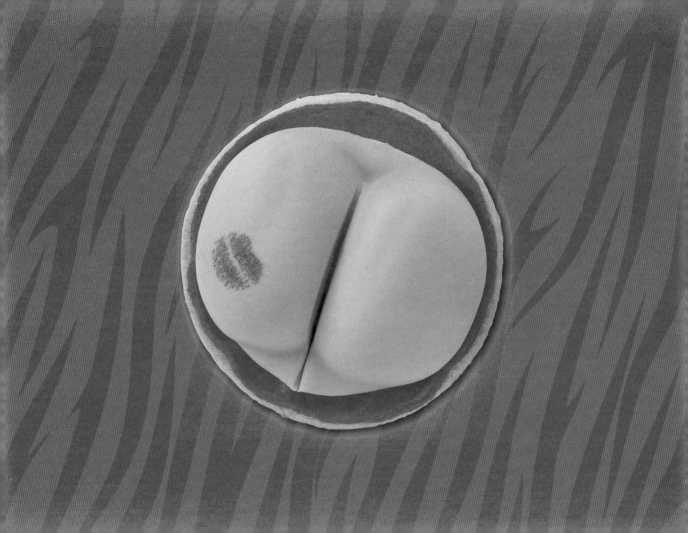

Fishnets

Butter, for greasing • 1 quantity Vanilla Cookie Dough (see page 8) • Flour, for dusting • 200 g (7 oz) royal icing sugar • Purple and black food colourings

One: Trace the Fishnets shape on page 93 and use to make a template. Preheat the oven to 190°C (375°F), Gas Mark 5 and grease a large baking sheet. Roll out the cookie dough on a lightly floured surface to a thickness of 5 mm (¼ inch). Cut out shapes by cutting round the template with a sharp knife or scalpel, rerolling the trimmings to make extra shapes.

Two: Space the cookies slightly apart on the baking sheet and bake in the preheated oven for about 15 minutes until turning golden around the edges. Leave the cookies on the baking sheet for 2 minutes to harden a little, then transfer to a wire rack to cool completely.

Three: Put the royal icing sugar in a bowl and add enough water, about 2 tablespoons, to mix to a smooth paste. Spoon 4 tablespoons into a separate bowl and beat in the purple food colouring. Place half the purple icing in a piping bag fitted with a writing nozzle and cover the rest tightly with clingfilm to prevent a crust forming.

Four: Beat black food colouring into the remaining icing and place in a piping bag fitted with a writing nozzle. Pipe 2 lines of black icing, 5 mm (¼ inch) apart, for the tops of the stockings. Pipe diagonal lines of black icing, first in one direction then the other, to make the fishnet stockings, then pipe further lines around the edges of the stockings.

Five: Use purple icing to pipe an outline for the shoes (scrape away any black icing first if it's gone into the shoe area). Pipe squiggly lines of purple icing between the black bands at the tops of the stockings. Add suspenders using both black and purple icing, finishing with piped dots to create simple flower shapes.

Six: Add a dash of water to the remaining purple icing to give a looser consistency. Put in a piping bag and snip off the tip so the icing flows quite freely. Use to fill in the shoes, easing the icing into the corners with a cocktail stick.

Food of Love

Butter, for greasing • 1 quantity Vanilla Cookie Dough (see page 8) • Flour, for dusting
• 1 quantity Vanilla Buttercream (see page 9) • Icing sugar, for dusting • 250 g (8 oz) red ready-to-roll icing
• 50 g (2 oz) green ready-to-roll icing • 150 g (5 oz) plain chocolate, melted (see page 10)

One: One: Preheat the oven to 190°C (375°F), Gas Mark 5 and grease a large baking sheet. Roll out the cookie dough on a lightly floured surface to a thickness of 5 mm (¼ inch). Cut out hearts using a 6 cm (2½ inch) heart-shaped cutter, rerolling the trimmings to make extra shapes.

Two: Space the cookies slightly apart on the baking sheet and bake in the preheated oven for about 15 minutes until turning golden around the edges. Leave the cookies on the baking sheet for 2 minutes to harden a little, then transfer to a wire rack to cool completely.

Three: Put one-third of the buttercream into a piping bag fitted with a writing nozzle. Spread the remaining buttercream over the cookies. Dust a work surface with icing sugar and roll out the red icing to a thickness of about 2.5 mm (⅛ inch). Cut out hearts using the cutter and press gently on to the cookies. Use the end of a fine paintbrush held at an angle of 45° to mark deep holes over the surfaces. Pipe tiny dots of buttercream into the holes for the pips.

Four: Line a tray or baking sheet with baking parchment and place the cookies on it. Roll out the green icing and cut out little diamond shapes for the leaves, 6 for each cookie. Brush the backs with a dampened paintbrush and press on to the cookies. Roll the trimmings under your fingers to make a long, thin sausage and cut into 2 cm (¾ inch) lengths for stalks. Secure in place and leave to harden for a couple of hours.

Five: Holding a cookie at an angle, drizzle melted chocolate over the top edge so it runs slightly down the strawberries. Return to the parchment and spoon a little puddle of melted chocolate along the base. Repeat with the rest of the cookies and leave to set.

Pin Up

Butter, for greasing • 1 quantity Vanilla Cookie Dough (see page 8) • Flour, for dusting • 1 quantity Vanilla Buttercream (see page 9) • Icing sugar, for dusting • 300 g (10 oz) white ready-to-roll icing • Blue, black, red and flesh-coloured food colourings

One: Preheat the oven to 190°C (375°F), Gas Mark 5 and grease a large baking sheet. Roll out the cookie dough on a lightly floured surface to a thickness of 5 mm (¼ inch). Cut out rectangles measuring 12x6 cm (5x2 inches), rerolling the trimmings to make extra shapes.

Two: Space the cookies slightly apart on the baking sheet and bake in the preheated oven for about 15 minutes until turning golden around the edges. Leave the cookies on the baking sheet for 2 minutes to harden a little, then transfer to a wire rack to cool completely.

Three: Spread the cookies almost to the edges with buttercream. Dust a work surface with icing sugar and roll out the white icing to a thickness of about 2.5 mm (⅛ inch). Cut out rectangles measuring 12x6 cm (5x2 inches), rerolling the trimmings to make extra shapes if necessary. Lay over the cookies and press down gently. Leave to harden for several hours or overnight.

Four: Trace the Pin Up Girl shape on page 93 and cut out to make a template. Dilute a little blue food colouring with water. Rest the template over a cookie and paint around the template with a fine paintbrush. Don't make the brush too wet or the colour will run under the template. Repeat on the remaining cookies.

Five: Paint the hair on the cookies with black food colouring and the bikini with blue colouring. Thin the flesh colouring with water and use to paint the skin. Add facial features and nail varnish with black, blue and red colourings.

Cabaret

Butter, for greasing • 1 quantity Hot Spice Cookie Dough (see page 95) • Flour, for dusting • Red colouring powder • 4 tablespoons granulated sugar • 1 quantity Vanilla Buttercream (see page 9) • Yellow food colouring • Icing sugar, for dusting • 100 g (3½ oz) black ready-to-roll icing • Confectioner's glaze or clear honey • Edible silver dusting powder • Drop of vegetable oil

One: Preheat the oven to 190°C (375°F), Gas Mark 5 and grease a large baking sheet. Roll out the cookie dough on a lightly floured surface to a thickness of 5 mm (¼ inch). Cut out hearts using a 6 cm (2½ inch) heart-shaped cutter, rerolling the trimmings to make extra shapes.

Two: Space the cookies slightly apart on the baking sheet and bake in the preheated oven for about 15 minutes until deep golden around the edges. Leave the cookies on the baking sheet for 2 minutes to harden a little, then transfer to a wire rack to cool completely.

Three: Add a little red colouring powder to the granulated sugar and work the colour into the granulated sugar with the back of a teaspoon. Once the colour is mostly distributed, use your fingers to rub the rest of the colour in. Scatter the sugar on a plate. Colour the buttercream with yellow food colouring and use about two-thirds of it to spread over the cookies. Press the buttercream into the coloured sugar until evenly coated.

Four: Trace the Cabaret shape on page 95 and cut out to make a template. Dust a work surface with icing sugar and roll out the black icing to a thickness of about 2.5 mm (⅛ inch). Cut out shapes by cutting round the template with a sharp knife or scalpel, rerolling the trimmings to make extra shapes if necessary. Brush the backs of the hats with a dampened paintbrush then position them on the cookies. Cut thin strips of icing from the trimmings to make hat bands, then stick in place on the hats.

Five: Put the remaining buttercream in a piping bag and snip off the tip so the icing can be piped in large dots. Pipe dots round the edges of the cookies. (If the buttercream doesn't stick to the sugar, press holes into the sugar with the handle end of a paintbrush and try again.) Roll the black icing trimmings under your fingers into lengths that taper almost to a point at one end. Trim into 9 cm (3½ inch) lengths and place on the cookies. Blend a little silver dusting powder with the oil to give a paint-like consistency. Use a small paintbrush to paint the tops on the canes.

Breathe In

Butter, for greasing • 1 quantity Vanilla Cookie Dough (see page 8) • Flour, for dusting • 300 g (10 oz) royal icing sugar • 2 teaspoons vanilla extract • Icing sugar, for dusting • 50 g (2 oz) grey ready-to-roll icing • 25 g (1 oz) white ready-to-roll icing • Black food colouring • Tube of black writing icing

One: Trace the Breathe In shape on page 94 and use to make a template. Preheat the oven to 190°C (375°F), Gas Mark 5 and grease a large baking sheet. Roll out the cookie dough on a lightly floured surface to a thickness of 5 mm (¼ inch). Cut out shapes by cutting round the template with a sharp knife or scalpel, rerolling the trimmings to make extra shapes.

Two: Space the cookies slightly apart on the baking sheet and bake in the preheated oven for about 15 minutes until turning golden around the edges. Leave the cookies on the baking sheet for 2 minutes to harden a little, then transfer to a wire rack to cool completely.

Three: Put the royal icing sugar in a bowl and add the vanilla extract and enough water, about 2½ tablespoons, to mix to a smooth paste. Put about one-quarter into a piping bag fitted with a writing nozzle and cover the rest tightly with clingfilm to prevent a crust forming. Dust a work surface with icing sugar and roll the grey icing to a thickness of about 2.5 mm (⅛ inch). Cut into 5 mm (¼ inch) strips. Ruffle one side of each strip (see page 11).

Pipe a line of icing along the top and bottom edges of each cookie and stick the ruffles in place at the edge of the cookies. Trim off the excess at the sides. Make white ruffles in the same way and position over the grey, securing with a dampened paintbrush.

Four: Use the black food colouring to make the remaining royal icing grey. Put one-third in a piping bag with a thin nozzle. Pipe lines around the edges of the cookies, overlapping the ruffles at top and bottom. Add a little water to the remaining grey icing to give a slightly looser consistency. Put in a piping bag and snip off the tip so the icing flows quite freely. Use to fill in the centres of the corsets, easing the icing into the corners with a cocktail stick. Leave to set for several hours or overnight.

Five: Use the bag of white icing to pipe the lace trim and ribbons. (If the icing has set in the nozzle, spoon the icing from the bag into a bowl while you fit another bag with the cleaned nozzle). Finally use the tube of black writing icing to make dots along the top and bottom edges.

Pole Dancer

Butter, for greasing • 1 quantity Chocolate Cookie Dough (see page 8) • Flour, for dusting • 50 g (2 oz) milk chocolate, melted (see page 10) • 300 g (10 oz) plain chocolate, melted (see page 10) • 1 quantity White Chocolate Ganache (see page 9) • Confectioner's glaze or clear honey (optional)

One: Preheat the oven to 190°C (375°F), Gas Mark 5 and grease a large baking sheet. Roll out the cookie dough on a lightly floured surface to a thickness of 5 mm (¼ inch). Cut out rectangles measuring 7.5x6.5 cm (3¼x2¾ inches), rerolling the trimmings to make extra shapes.

Two: Space the cookies slightly apart on the baking sheet and bake in the preheated oven for about 15 minutes until turning darker around the edges. Leave the cookies on the baking sheet for 2 minutes to harden a little, then transfer to a wire rack to cool completely.

Three: Trace the Pole Dancer shape on page 00 and cut out to make a template. Line a tray or large baking sheet with baking parchment and slide the template under the parchment. Put the milk chocolate in a piping bag and snip off the merest tip. Pipe round the outline of the pole, then fill in the pole with more piping.

Four: Put the plain chocolate in a piping bag and snip off the merest tip. Use to pipe round the outline of the dancer. Slide the template along under the parchment and pipe more poles and dancers in the same way. Snip off a little more of the plain chocolate piping bag and use to fill in the dancers, easing the chocolate into the corners with a cocktail stick. Leave to set for several hours.

Five: Spread the cookies with chocolate ganache. Carefully peel the parchment away from the chocolate shapes and gently rest them on the cookies. Brush confectioner's glaze or clear honey over the figures, if using.

Pussy Galore

300 g (10 oz) royal icing sugar • Black and orange food colourings • Butter, for greasing
• 1 quantity Hot Spice Cookie Dough (see page 8) • Flour, for dusting
• 1 quantity Vanilla Buttercream (see page 9) • Confectioner's glaze or clear honey (optional)

One: Trace the Pussy Galore shape on page 93 and cut out to make a template. Line a tray or large baking sheet with baking parchment and slide the template under the parchment. Put the royal icing sugar in a bowl and add enough water, about 3 tablespoons, to mix to a smooth paste. Beat in the black food colouring and spoon a third of the icing into a piping bag fitted with a writing nozzle and cover the rest tightly with clingfilm to prevent a crust forming.

Two: Use the icing to pipe round the outline of the shape. Slide the template along under the parchment and pipe outlines in the same way. Add a dash of water to the remaining icing to give a slightly looser consistency. Put in a piping bag and snip off the tip so the icing flows quite freely. Use to fill in the centres of the shapes, easing the icing into the corners with a cocktail stick. Leave to set for 2 days.

Three: Preheat the oven to 190°C (375°F), Gas Mark 5 and grease a large baking sheet. Roll out the cookie dough on a lightly floured surface to a thickness of 5 mm (¼ inch). Cut out rounds using a 7 cm (3 inch) cutter, rerolling the trimmings to make extra shapes.

Four: Space the cookies slightly apart on the baking sheet and bake in the preheated oven for about 15 minutes until deep golden around the edges. Leave the cookies on the baking sheet for 2 minutes to harden a little, then transfer to a wire rack to cool completely.

Five: Colour the buttercream deep orange and spread over the cookies. Carefully peel the parchment away from the icing figures and rest them gently on the cookies. Brush confectioner's glaze or clear honey over the figures, if using.

Whip It Up

Butter, for greasing • 1 quantity Hot Spice Cookie Dough (see page 8) • Flour, for dusting
• 300 g (10 oz) royal icing sugar • Deep red food colouring • 400 g (13 oz) black ready-to-roll icing
• Icing sugar, for dusting • Tube of black writing icing • Confectioner's glaze or clear honey
• Edible silver dusting powder • Drop of vegetable oil

One: Preheat the oven to 190°C (375°F), Gas Mark 5 and grease a large baking sheet. Roll out the cookie dough on a lightly floured surface to a thickness of 5 mm (¼ inch). Cut out stars using a 7.5 cm (3¼ inch) star-shaped cutter, rerolling the trimmings for extra shapes.

Two: Space the cookies slightly apart on the baking sheet and bake in the preheated oven for about 15 minutes until deep golden around the edges. Leave the cookies on the baking sheet for 2 minutes to harden a little, then transfer to a wire rack to cool completely.

Three: Put the royal icing sugar in a bowl and beat in 3–4 tablespoons of water to give a consistency that thickly coats the back of the spoon. Beat in the red food colouring. Place the wire rack of cookies over a large sheet of paper and spoon the icing over the stars to coat completely. Leave to set for several hours.

Four: Take a 15 g (½ oz) piece of black icing. Using hands dusted with icing sugar, mould it into a flat disc about 3.5 cm (1½ inches) in diameter. Take a similar-sized piece and shape into a slightly larger, flatter disc for the top of the hat. Moisten the back with a dampened paintbrush and secure on top of the first disc. Take a smaller piece of icing and flatten into an oval shape, measuring about 3x1.5 cm (1¼x¾ inch). Cut off one long edge and secure to the bottom of the cap. Transfer to a sheet of baking parchment and make the remainder in the same way. Use the black icing to pipe a row of dots along the fronts of the caps for braid.

Five: Roll a little more icing under your fingers to make a long, thin sausage about 2.5 mm (⅛ inch) thick. Cut into 3.5 cm (1½ inch) lengths to make the whip handles. Transfer to the baking parchment. Cut off any icing that has set under the cookies so they sit flat. Roll the remaining black icing as thinly as possible and arrange in loops on the cookies, painting the handles at the ends, with a dampened paintbrush. Arrange the caps next to them. Use the confectioner's glaze or honey (diluted if thick with hot water) to brush over the caps. Blend a little silver dusting powder with the oil for a paint-like consistency. Paint silver over the braid with a small brush.

Black Panther

Butter, for greasing • 1 quantity Hot Spice Cookie Dough (see page 8)
• Flour, for dusting • 200 g (7 oz) plain chocolate, melted (see page 10)
• Edible silver balls

One: Trace the Black Panther shape on page 95 and use to make a template. Preheat the oven to 190°C (375°F), Gas Mark 5 and grease a large baking sheet. Roll out the cookie dough on a lightly floured surface to a thickness of 5 mm (¼ inch). Cut out shapes by cutting round the template with a sharp knife or scalpel, rerolling the trimmings to make extra shapes.

Two: Space the cookies slightly apart on the baking sheet and bake in the preheated oven for about 15 minutes until deep golden around the edges. Leave the cookies on the baking sheet for 2 minutes to harden a little, then transfer to a wire rack to cool completely.

Three: Line a tray or baking sheet with baking parchment. Spoon the chocolate over the cookies, spreading it to coat entirely and letting the excess chocolate drip back into the bowl. Scrape off the drips from around the edges of the cookies and transfer to the tray. While the chocolate is still soft, gently press a row of silver balls on to the cookies to resemble a collar.

Unbuttoned

Butter, for greasing • 1 quantity Chocolate Cookie Dough (see page 8) • Flour, for dusting • 1 quantity White Chocolate Ganache (see page 9) • Icing sugar, for dusting • 250 g (8 oz) flesh-coloured ready-to-roll icing • Black and flesh-coloured food colourings • 500 g (1 lb) blue ready-to-roll icing • Edible silver dusting powder • Drop of vegetable oil

One: Preheat the oven to 190°C (375°F), Gas Mark 5 and grease a large baking sheet. Roll out the cookie dough on a lightly floured surface to a thickness of 5 mm (¼ inch). Cut out rounds using a 7.5 cm (3¼ inch) cutter, rerolling the trimmings to make extra shapes.

Two: Space the cookies slightly apart on the baking sheet and bake in the preheated oven for about 15 minutes until turning darker around the edges. Leave the cookies on the baking sheet for 2 minutes to harden a little, then transfer to a wire rack to` cool completely.

Three: Spread the cookies with chocolate ganache. Divide the flesh-coloured icing into equal pieces, one for each cookie. Dust a work surface with icing sugar, take one piece of icing and shape it to resemble a man's torso. Once you've made the basic shape, cut the bottom edge, leaving a protruding V-shape in the middle. Use a cocktail stick to make a belly button and the side of a fine paintbrush to impress '6 pack' markings in the icing.

Four: Knead black food colouring into the blue icing to made a dark denim colour. Take a 40 g (1½ oz) piece, mould into a flat square and make a cut from one edge to the centre. Open out the cut and smooth out the edges. Cut a V-shape into the top edge and slot it on to the torso. Complete the markings on the jeans, adding creases, flies and pockets. Slice off the icing at the top and bottom with a knife and position on a cookie. Make the remainder in the same way.

Five: Roll thin strips of blue icing and secure around the waists of the jeans. Add tiny buttons and belt loops. Use diluted flesh colouring and a fine paintbrush to add definition to the torso and diluted black colouring to add darker areas to the jeans. Paint stitches with black food colouring. Blend a little silver dusting powder with the oil to give a paint-like consistency. Use a small paintbrush to paint silver over the buttons.

Beyond Feathers

Butter, for greasing • 1 quantity Hot Spice Cookie Dough (see page 8) • Flour, for dusting • 2 quantities Vodka Buttercream (see page 9) • Black, red and orange food colourings

One: Preheat the oven to 190°C (375°F), Gas Mark 5 and grease a large baking sheet. Roll out the cookie dough on a lightly floured surface to a thickness of 5 mm (¼ inch). Cut out 2 rounds measuring 14 cm (5½ inches) in diameter, using a small plate as a guide. Cut each round into 4 quarters, then reroll the trimmings, cut out a semi-circle of the same diameter and cut it in half.

Two: Space the cookies slightly apart on the baking sheet and bake in the preheated oven for about 15 minutes until deep golden around the edges. Leave the cookies on the baking sheet for 2 minutes to harden a little, then transfer to a wire rack to cool completely.

Three: Spoon 2 tablespoons of the buttercream into a separate bowl, beat in the black food colouring and put it in a piping bag. Snip off the merest tip and use to pipe lines for the bases of the feathers. Add orange food colouring to two-thirds of the remaining buttercream and red colouring to the remainder. Place in piping bags and snip off the merest tips.

Four: Use the orange buttercream to pipe slightly curved lines from the black lines to the edges of the fans. Pipe short diagonal lines on each side of these to resemble feathers. Take the red buttercream and pipe further lines over the initial feather lines. Use the remaining red buttercream to add more diagonal lines near the tops of the fans. Pipe a dot of red buttercream at the base of each fan.

In the Beginning

Butter, for greasing • 1 quantity Hot Spice Cookie Dough (see page 8) • Flour, for dusting • 1 egg white, beaten • 1 quantity Vodka Buttercream (see page 9) • Icing sugar, for dusting • 50 g (2 oz) green ready-to-roll icing • Small piece of blue ready-to-roll icing • Tube of red writing icing

One: Preheat the oven to 190°C (375°F), Gas Mark 5 and grease a large baking sheet. Roll out the cookie dough on a lightly floured surface to a thickness of 5 mm (¼ inch). Cut out shapes using an 8 or 9-cm (3¼ or 3½ inch) gingerbread man cutter, rerolling the trimmings to make extra shapes. Join the figures in pairs by cutting a small slice off two arms and feet, brushing the cut edges with beaten egg white and pushing them firmly together on the baking sheet.

Two: Bake in the preheated oven for about 15 minutes until deep golden around the edges. Leave the cookies on the baking sheet for 2 minutes to harden a little, then transfer to a wire rack to cool completely.

Three: Put the buttercream in a piping bag fitted with a writing nozzle. Dust a work surface with icing sugar and roll out the green icing to a thickness of about 2.5 mm (⅛ inch). Cut out 10 of the larger leaves for each cookie using a cutter or by cutting out small diamond shapes by hand. Stick in place with buttercream, using the picture as a guide.

Four: Pipe long hair on to the female figures and shorter hair on to the male figures. Cut out smaller leaves, about 14 per cookie, and secure around the heads. Pipe eyes with buttercream, adding tiny balls of blue icing for the centres. Finally, pipe the mouths using the tube of red icing.

French Maid

Butter, for greasing • 1 quantity Hot Spice Cookie Dough (see page 8) • Flour, for dusting • 1 quantity Vanilla Buttercream (see page 9) • Icing sugar, for dusting • 200 g (7 oz) pink ready-to-roll icing • 75 g (3 oz) black ready-to-roll icing • Tubes of white and black writing icing • Small piece of white ready-to-roll icing

One: Preheat the oven to 190°C (375°F), Gas Mark 5 and grease a large baking sheet. Roll out the cookie dough on a lightly floured surface to a thickness of 5 mm (¼ inch). Cut out rounds using a 7.5 cm (3¼ inch) cutter, rerolling the trimmings to make extra shapes.

Two: Space the cookies slightly apart on the baking sheet and bake in the preheated oven for about 15 minutes until deep golden around the edges. Leave the cookies on the baking sheet for 2 minutes to harden a little, then transfer to a wire rack to cool completely.

Three: Spread the cookies almost to the edges with buttercream. Dust a work surface with icing sugar and roll out the pink icing to a thickness of about 2.5 mm (⅛ inch). Cut out rounds using the 7.5 cm (3¼ inch) cutter. Position on the cookies and press down gently.

Four: Trace the French Maid shape on page 92 and cut out to make a template. Thinly roll out the black icing and cut out shapes by cutting round the template with a sharp knife or scalpel, rerolling the trimmings to make extra shapes. Ruffle the lower edges of the outfits (see page 00). Paint the backs with a dampened paintbrush and lay on the cookies. Lift the ruffled edges and pipe wiggly lines of white and black writing icing to resemble frilly underskirts.

Five: Thinly roll out the white icing and cut out the fronts and aprons. Secure in place. Use white writing icing to pipe the blouse and black writing icing to finish the decoration. For the feather dusters, roll out the black icing trimmings under your fingers to make a long, thin sausage about 3 mm (⅛ inch) thick and cut into 2.5-cm (1-inch) lengths. Position on the cookies, adding a small ball of black icing to the end of each. Finally, pipe the feathers in white icing.

Pop Your Cork

Butter, for greasing • 1 quantity Chocolate Cookie Dough (see page 8) • Flour, for dusting • 1 quantity Chocolate Ganache (see page 9) • Icing sugar, for dusting • 100 g (3½ oz) deep green ready-to-roll icing • Small piece each of white and pale brown ready-to-roll icings • 50 g (2 oz) white chocolate, melted (see page 10) • Tube of black writing icing • 1 small sheet of gold leaf

One: Preheat the oven to 190°C (375°F), Gas Mark 5 and grease a large baking sheet. Roll out the cookie dough on a lightly floured surface to a thickness of 5 mm (¼ inch). Cut into 8 cm (3¼ inch) squares, rerolling the trimmings to make extra shapes.

Two: Space the cookies slightly apart on the baking sheet and bake in the preheated oven for about 15 minutes until turning darker around the edges. Leave the cookies on the baking sheet for 2 minutes to harden a little, then transfer to a wire rack to cool completely.

Three: Spread the cookies to the edges with chocolate ganache. Trace the Pop Your Cork shape on page 92 and cut out to make a template. Dust a work surface with icing sugar and thinly roll out the green icing. Cut out shapes by cutting round the template with a sharp knife or scalpel, rerolling the trimmings to make extra shapes.

Four: Position the bottles in the corners of the cookies. Roll out the white icing and cut into small rectangles for labels. Brush the backs with a dampened paintbrush and position on the bottles, trimming off the excess that overhangs the bottom edge. Mould tiny mushroom-shapes in brown icing for corks and press gently into the ganache.

Five: Put the white chocolate in a piping bag and snip off the merest tip. Use to pipe bubbles coming out of the bottles. Use black icing to decorate the label. Dampen the bottle neck with water using a fine paintbrush. Tear the gold leaf into small pieces using tweezers or cocktail sticks and stick to the bottle neck.

Bleeding Heart

Butter, for greasing • 1 quantity Vanilla Cookie Dough (see page 8)
• Flour, for dusting • 300 g (10 oz) royal icing sugar • 2 teaspoons vanilla extract
• Red food colouring • Edible silver dusting powder • Drop of vegetable oil

One: Preheat the oven to 190°C (375°F), Gas Mark 5 and grease a large baking sheet. Roll out the cookie dough on a lightly floured surface to a thickness of 5 mm (¼ inch). Cut out hearts using a 7 cm (3 inch) heart-shaped cutter, rerolling the trimmings to make extra shapes.

Two: Space the cookies slightly apart on the baking sheet and bake in the preheated oven for about 15 minutes until turning golden around the edges. Leave the cookies on the baking sheet for 2 minutes to harden a little, then transfer to a wire rack to cool completely.

Three: Put the royal icing sugar in a bowl and add the vanilla extract and enough water, about 2½ tablespoons, to mix to a smooth paste. Beat in the red food colouring. Put 4 tablespoons of the icing into a piping bag fitted with a writing nozzle and cover the rest tightly with clingfilm to prevent a crust forming. Pipe the red icing around the edges of the cookies. When you get to the pointed tip of each heart, pipe several teardrop shapes to resemble drops of blood.

Four: Transfer 2 tablespoons of the remaining icing to a small bowl, cover tightly with clingfilm and set aside. Add a dash of water to the icing in the larger bowl to give a slightly looser consistency. Put in another piping bag and snip off the tip so the icing flows quite freely. Use to fill in the centres of the hearts and the drops, easing the icing into the corners with a cocktail stick. Leave to set for several hours or overnight.

Five: Put the reserved icing in a piping bag fitted with a writing nozzle and pipe on the barbed wire across the hearts. Leave to harden. Blend a little silver dusting powder with the oil to give a paint-like consistency. Use a small paintbrush to paint silver over the barbed wire.

Looking For An Egg

Butter, for greasing • 1 quantity Vanilla Cookie Dough (see page 8) • Flour, for dusting
• 1 quantity Vanilla Buttercream (see page 9) • Black food colouring • Icing sugar, for dusting
• 25 g (1 oz) white ready-to-roll icing • Tubes of red and black writing icing

One: Trace the Looking For An Egg shape on page 94 and use to make a template. Preheat the oven to 190°C (375°F), Gas Mark 5 and grease a large baking sheet. Roll out the cookie dough on a lightly floured surface to a thickness of 5 mm (¼ inch). Cut out shapes by cutting round the template with a sharp knife or scalpel, rerolling the trimmings to make extra shapes.

Two: Space the cookies slightly apart on the baking sheet and bake in the preheated oven for about 15 minutes until turning golden around the edges. Leave the cookies on the baking sheet for 2 minutes to harden a little, then transfer to a wire rack to cool completely.

Three: Colour the buttercream grey using a dash of black food colouring. Use a palette knife to spread over the cookies in a flat layer, scraping off the excess around the edges. Use a cocktail stick or skewer to mark small wavy lines in the icing on the tail ends.

Four: Dust your fingers with icing sugar and take a pea-sized ball of white icing. Flatten it between finger and thumb and press gently into the buttercream to make an eye. Repeat with the other eyes. Use black food colouring and a fine paintbrush to paint the centres of the eyes. Pipe the mouths with red writing icing, and eyebrows with black writing icing.

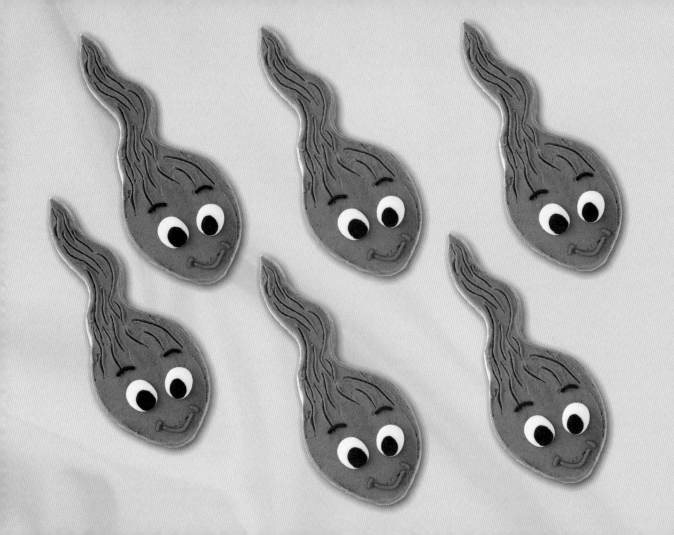

Sexy Slippers

Icing sugar, for dusting • 75 g (3 oz) pale pink ready-to-roll icing • Butter, for greasing • 1 quantity Chocolate Cookie Dough (see page 8) • Flour, for dusting • 1 quantity Chocolate Ganache (see page 9) • Pink food colouring • 1 quantity Vanilla Buttercream (see page 9)

One: Line a tray or baking sheet with baking parchment. Trace the Sexy Slippers shapes on page 92 and cut out to make a template. Dust a work surface with icing sugar and thinly roll out the pink icing. Cut out shapes by cutting round the template with a sharp knife or scalpel, rerolling the trimmings to make extra shapes. Transfer to the tray and leave to harden for several hours or overnight.

Two: Preheat the oven to 190°C (375°F), Gas Mark 5 and grease a large baking sheet. Roll out the cookie dough on a lightly floured surface to a thickness of 5 mm (¼ inch). Cut out hearts using a 7 cm (3 inch) heart-shaped cutter, rerolling the trimmings to make extra shapes.

Three: Space the cookies slightly apart on the baking sheet and bake in the preheated oven for about 15 minutes until turning darker around the edges. Leave the cookies on the baking sheet for 2 minutes to harden a little, then transfer to a wire rack to cool completely.

Four: Spread the cookies with chocolate ganache. Use a fine paintbrush to paint the darker areas on the slippers with pink food colouring, then arrange the slippers on the cookies. Put the buttercream in a piping bag fitted with a writing nozzle and pipe around the edges of the slippers. Add the details, then finish by piping a large pom pom on each slipper.

Itsy Bitsy Pants

Butter, for greasing • 1 quantity Chocolate Cookie Dough (see page 8) • Flour, for dusting • 1 quantity Chocolate Ganache (see page 9) • Icing sugar, for dusting • 200 g (7 oz) pale brown ready-to-roll icing • 50 g (2 oz) black ready-to-roll icing • Small piece of dark brown ready-to-roll icing • Purple colouring powder • 3 tablespoons granulated sugar • 75 g (3 oz) purple ready-to-roll icing • Edible pink balls

One: Preheat the oven to 190°C (375°F), Gas Mark 5 and grease a large baking sheet. Roll out the cookie dough on a lightly floured surface to a thickness of 5 mm (¼ inch). Cut out rounds using a 7.5 cm (3¼ inch) cutter, rerolling the trimmings to make extra shapes.

Two: Space the cookies slightly apart on the baking sheet and bake in the preheated oven for about 15 minutes until turning darker around the edges. Leave the cookies on the baking sheet for 2 minutes to harden a little, then transfer to a wire rack to cool completely.

Three: Spread the cookies with chocolate ganache, leaving a 1 cm (½ inch) border around the edges. Dust a work surface with icing sugar and roll out the pale brown icing to a thickness of about 2.5 mm (⅛ inch). Break off tiny balls of black icing, flatten them slightly and press gently into the pale brown icing, spacing them slightly apart. Vary the size of the balls a little to add interest. Take smaller balls of dark brown icing and place on top of the larger black balls. Gently roll with the rolling pin to incorporate the three icings. Cut out rounds using the 7.5 cm (3¼ inch) cutter and press them gently on to the cookies.

Four: Add a little purple colouring powder to the granulated sugar and work the colour into the sugar with the back of a teaspoon. Once the colour is mostly distributed, use your fingers to rub the rest of the colour in. Scatter the sugar on a plate.

Five: Roll out the purple icing thinly and cut out skimpy thong shapes with a sharp knife or scalpel. Place on the sugar and press down gently to completely coat one side. Brush the backs with a dampened paintbrush and position on the cookies. Use the purple icing trimmings to shape bows with trailing ribbons. Secure in place and decorate with edible pink balls.

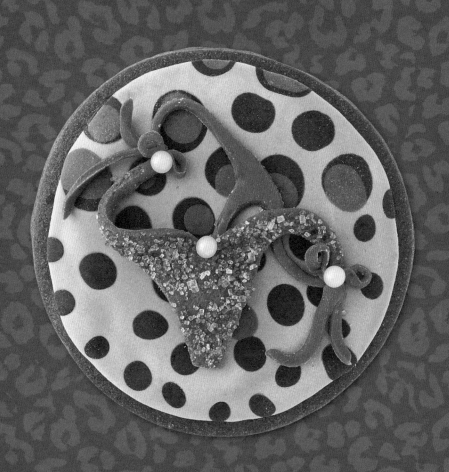

Venus and Mars

1 quantity Vanilla Cookie Dough (see page 8) • Flour, for dusting • 1 egg white, beaten • 75 g (3 oz) clear red boiled sweets, roughly crushed • 200 g (7 oz) royal icing sugar • Black and red food colourings • Edible red glitter

One: Preheat the oven to 190°C (375°F), Gas Mark 5 and line a large baking sheet with baking parchment. Roll out the cookie dough on a lightly floured surface to a thickness of 5 mm (¼ inch). Cut out rounds using a 5 cm (2 inch) cutter, then cut out the centres using a 3 cm (1¼ inch) cutter. Overlap two circles, cutting away the areas that overlap so the circles can be joined together.

Two: Brush the cut edges with beaten egg white and push the pairs of circles firmly together on the baking sheet. Reroll the trimmings and cut out a cross-shape and an arrow shape for each cookie using a sharp knife. Brush one edge with egg white and attach to the cross shape and do the same to the other side to attach the arrow.

Three: Bake in the preheated oven for 5 minutes. Place a few pieces of crushed sweet into the holes in the cookies and return to the oven for 6–8 minutes or until the cookies are turning golden around the edges. If necessary, use a cocktail stick to spread the melted syrup into any areas that haven't been filled, then leave to cool completely on the baking sheet.

Four: Put the royal icing sugar in a bowl and add enough water, about 2 tablespoons, to mix to a smooth paste. Divide between two bowls and add red food colouring to one bowl and black to the other. Put a little of the black icing into a piping bag fitted with a writing nozzle and cover the rest tightly with clingfilm to prevent a crust forming. Repeat with the red icing.

Five: Pipe around the edges of the male (arrow) symbols in black icing and the female (cross) symbols in red. Add a dash of water to the remaining icings to give a slightly looser consistency. Put in piping bags and snip off the tips so the icing flows quite freely. Use to fill in the centres of the shapes, easing the icing into the corners with a cocktail stick. Sprinkle the red icing with edible glitter while still soft.

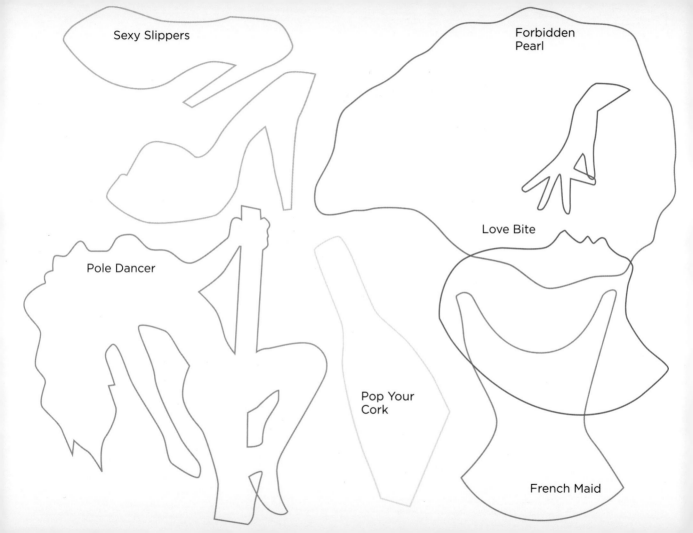

Sexy Slippers

Forbidden Pearl

Pole Dancer

Love Bite

Pop Your Cork

French Maid

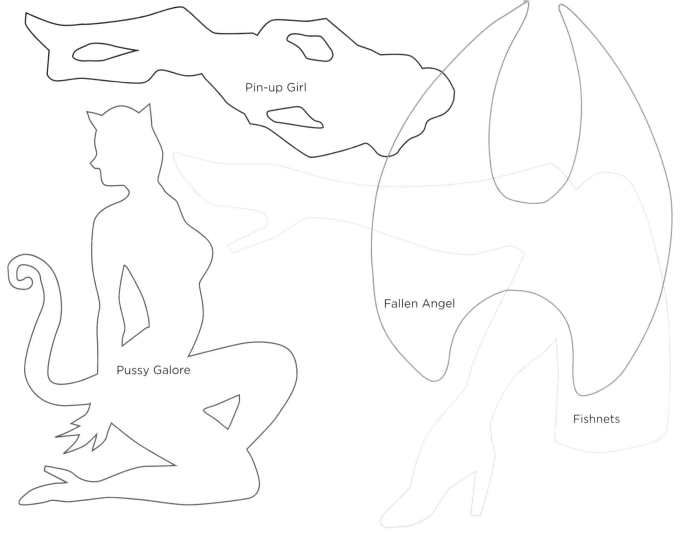

Pin-up Girl

Pussy Galore

Fallen Angel

Fishnets

Looking for an Egg

Breathe In

Long Lashes

Kinky Boots

Baby Doll

Heaven Scent

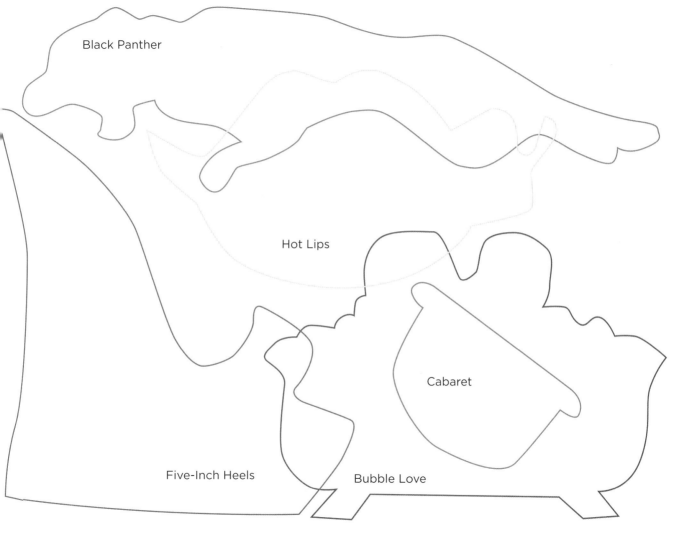

Black Panther

Hot Lips

Cabaret

Five-Inch Heels

Bubble Love

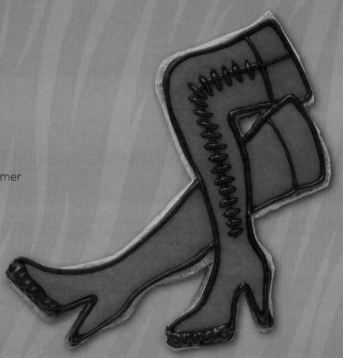

Acknowledgements

PUBLISHER: Sarah Ford

EDITOR: Jo Wilson

DESIGN MANAGER: Eoghan O'Brien

DESIGNER: Clare Barber

PRODUCTION CONTROLLER: Sarah Kramer

PROOFREADER: Keira Price

FOOD STYLIST: Joanna Farrow

PHOTOGRAPHER: Lis Parsons